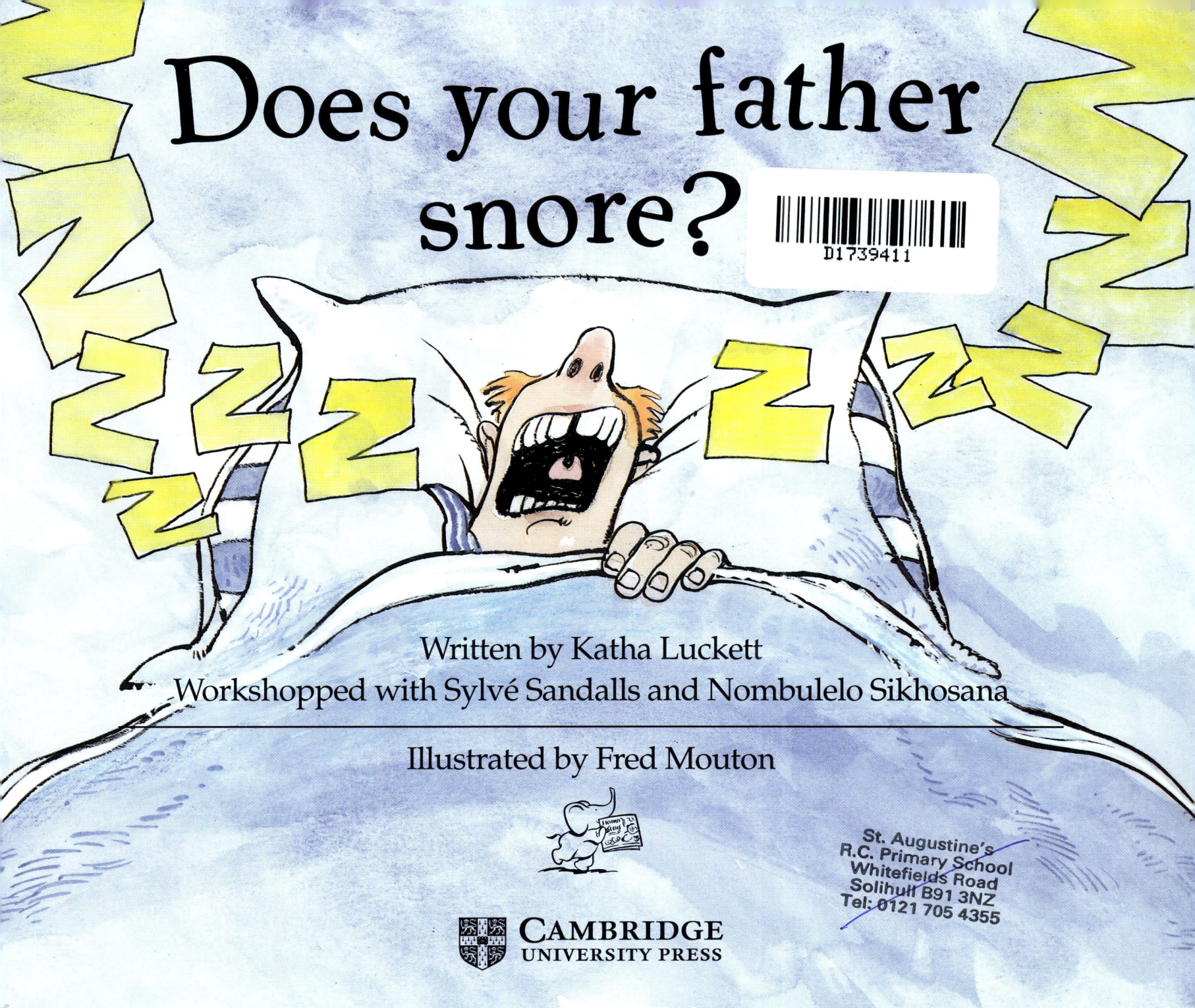

Does your father snore?

Written by Katha Luckett
Workshopped with Sylvé Sandalls and Nombulelo Sikhosana

Illustrated by Fred Mouton

CAMBRIDGE
UNIVERSITY PRESS

D1739411

Does *your* father snore? *Ours* did!
He snored as loudly as a hippo in water.
"Ghrrr! Ghrrr!", snored Father.

We tried everything but we could not sleep.
First we put our pillows over our heads.
"Ghrrr! Ghrrr!", snored Father.

3

"Please, Daddy, please don't snore!"
we begged him the next morning.
"What! Me? I don't snore!" said father.

4

The next night Father began to snore again.

"*Ghrrr! Ghrrr!*", snored Father.

This time we lay under our beds.

But we still could not sleep.

The following night we were very, very tired.
We made a plan. When father began to snore,
we tiptoed into his room. Carefully, we carried
Father outside.

We tucked his blankets around him
and crept back to bed.
Then we went to sleep at last.

In the yard, a big black spider
was spinning a thread – right over Father's head!
"Ghrrr! Ghrrr!" snored Father. His mouth was wide open.
The spider came lower and lower and lower...

... and fell right into father's mouth!

"*Yaah!*" yelled Father.

He jumped out of bed.

You can guess what happened next...

14

But father *never* slept with his mouth open again!